CW00853314

God, Does Humanity Exist?

Kamand Kojouri

Also by Kamand Kojouri:

The Eternal Dance: Love Poetry and Prose

Copyright © 2020 Kamand Kojouri

All rights reserved. No part of this book may be used or reproduced in any form or by any means, electronic or mechanical, including photocopying, recording, or by any information storage and retrieval system, without written permission from the author.

United Kingdom

ISBN: 1984949306
ISBN-13: 978-1984949301

Worry not
if you're in darkness
and the void draws you in.
This isn't the place we go to die for ever.
It's where we are reborn
and our stories begin.

CONTENTS

AUTHOR'S NOTE

The title of this book isn't meant to make us despair. Rather, it is meant to make us think…

For thousands of years people have asked the question, 'Does God exist?' But I believe what is much more elusive is the quality that is becoming rarer and harder to find—our humanity.

Like most children, I used to believe God was the sun. It made sense to me because the sun followed me wherever I went during the day, and its light continued to be reflected by the moon at night. I now know this isn't far from the truth. God is the light from the sun. The light that encourages the flower to open itself and offer its beauty to the world. The light that guides us in darkness and helps us find our way home. We all have a spark of this light within us, for we, all of us, live in God. And by sharing our light with others, it grows brighter and stronger.

The title of this book is meant to make us think, because whilst I assert the existence of an intangible, incomprehensible, and inexplicable God, I question the existence of humanity.

God, to me, isn't selective. I don't pray because I believe that God will grant my wishes. I pray because it is only then that I know what I want. It is then that I call out to the universe and every cell in my body that this is what I strive for, this is what I need and what I desire. I don't want to believe in a God who loves me more than others and listens to my prayers of wanting a scholarship but ignores the cries of the Syrian boy who is praying for his sister to live—even though he has just witnessed her limbs being torn apart in front of his very eyes.

In school, I was incorrectly introduced to God through fear. But I first came to truly know God through love. I have seen and felt God through Bach's partitas and Hafez's ghazals.

But I, too, have seen and felt humanity. I do not doubt its existence. But I pray that we think, speak, and act more humanely—with more compassion, empathy, and understanding. I pray that we can be the light for one another when all we see are shadows…

There is a large brick wall that is visible from the windows of my apartment in Swansea. In black and white it reads: *More poetry is needed*. I am reminded of this every single day. And it has now become my own mantra, because poetry raises our consciousness. It voices the common pain and cries out for a change.

When Nietzsche famously said, 'God is dead,' his aim was not to lead us to nihilistic beliefs, but rather to rescue us from them. Similarly, the title of this book is not meant to make us hopeless, but to make us think. It is also meant to make us act…

KK
14/03/2019

God, Does Humanity Exist?

I. CRIES OF COMMON PAIN

'[…] I am the common pain,
cry me out!'

Ahmad Shamlou

THEY WANT US TO BE AFRAID.
They want us to be afraid of leaving our homes,
to barricade our doors and hide our children.
They aim to make us fear life!

They want us to hate.
They want us to hate *the other*,
to practice aggression and perfect oppression.
They aim to divide us all!

They want us to be inhuman.
They want us to throw out our kindness,
to conceal our love and bury our hope.
They aim to take all our light!

They think their brick walls
will separate us.
They think their damned bombs
will defeat us.

They are so ignorant they don't understand
that my soul and your soul are old friends.
They are so ignorant they don't understand
that when they cut you, I bleed.

They are so ignorant they don't understand
that we will never be afraid,
we will never hate,
and we will never be silent.
Let life be only ours!

ref·u·gee noun: *a person who flees for refuge or safety*

We are, each of us, refugees
when we flee from burning buildings
into the arms of our loving families.
When we flee from floods and earthquakes
to sleep on vouchsafed mats in sanctuaries.
We are, each of us, refugees
when we flee from abusive relationships
or shooters in cinemas
and shopping centres.

Sometimes it only takes a day
for our countries to persecute us
because of our race, religion, or opinion.
Sometimes it only takes a minute
for the missiles to rain down
and leave our towns in ruin and destitution.

We are, each of us, refugees
longing for that amniotic tranquillity,
dreaming of freedom and safety
when fences and barbed wires
will spring into walled gardens.

Lebanese, Sudanese, Libyan and Syrian,
Yemeni, Somali, Palestinian, and Ethiopian,
like our brothers and sisters,
we are, each of us, refugees.
The bombs fell in their cafés and squares
where once poetry, dancing, and laughter prevailed.
Only their olive trees
remember music and merriment now
as their cities wail for departed children
without a funeral.

We are, each of us, refugees.
Don't let stamped paper tell you any differently.
We have been fleeing for centuries
because to stay means getting bullets in our heads.
Because to stay means being hanged by our necks.
Because to stay means being jailed, raped, and left
for dead.

But we can, each of us, be someone's refuge
so they don't board dinghies
when they can't swim.
So they don't climb walls
with snipers aimed at their chest.
So they don't choose to stay
and be killed instead.

When home turns into hell,
you, too, will run
with tears in your eyes screaming *rescue me!*
and then you'll know for certain:
    you've always been a refugee.

HEAVEN AND HELL

I don't know why it's still unclear
whether heaven and hell exist.
Do we need more evidence?
They lie right here—in our midst.
Heaven is standing on Mount Qasioun,
drinking Damascene scenes
as the jasmine breeze
carries Qabbani's verses
through trees of willow.
And Hell is only a four-hour ride
to Aleppo, where children's cries
drown the roars of mortar bombs
until they lose their families,
their limbs and tongues.
Yes, hell persists,
                    right here in our midst.
And all we do to extinguish this hellfire
is sigh, shrug, like, and share.
Do tell:
What does this make of us?
Are we any better
than *the gatekeepers of hell?*

FRIDAY

It is raining blood today.
I open my book and write **Black Lives Matter**
to acknowledge the unanswered injustices.
I write **Blue Lives Matter**,
for how can any human
be separate
from humanity?
I write **All Lives Matter**
but stare at these words—
Don't they invalidate the others?
              I stand conflicted
as the clouds continue to bleed.
I try to erase the last phrase
but find the blood
has already
drowned my words.

GOD IS NOT DEAD.
She has forsaken us.
We wipe our angry, hate-filled tears
after another shooting as a man
polishes his gun outside a mosque.
All those stolen lives—we scream
for justice! But God has quietly left
our temples and churches.
She will not return, for what *we* have done
is much worse. We have murdered
                              humanity.
God has deserted even the devoutest of us—
those who hoard our love and compassion
only for the good and righteous as we abandon
the bigots brimming with hate.
Yes, they are the least deserving of love
but the most in need of it.
God's agony rings in our hearts.
She wails for the future
                      shooters.
And though we reject them,
God greets these cracked and confused creatures—
the least deserving of compassion
but the most in need of it!
These suggestible souls susceptible
to the systematic vitriol spilling
from demagogues and cult leaders,
brainwashing them.
We read their spiteful tweets,
yet when we pass them in classrooms,
in trains and markets,
we dismiss those seemingly small, nameless
opportunities for kindness.

We don't know—and how ignorant we are—
that every time
we ignore them,
we sharpen our daggers
and butcher humanity in its raw flesh—
not in dark alleyways, no, but in the light of day.
Because hating them,
shows how loving we are.
Because condemning them,
proves how moral we are.
And every shooting illuminates
the collapse of our collective duty
to love as God loves,
to be compassionate as God
is compassionate.
                    Prayers heal, yes—
but for God's sake, let God be.
                              First,
let's resurrect our humanity.

IN MEMORIAM: FLIGHT 752

I try to envisage the passengers
seated in neat rows.
Everyone knows the real risk
is at take-off and landing,
but after an hour delay,
their plane was soaring. Relieved,
they whispered prayers, dreaming
of families and friends at arrival gates
clutching coffee cups and bouquets.
I like to think it was calm,
the plane blanketed by night's caress.
Cellphones put away,
the cabin lights dimmed,
babies cooing in cots,
and refreshments on their way.
176 hearts beating in one narrow womb.
                    Closer to the heavens,
I know their journey was short—
earth angels for a while
who were returning home.

SOME PEOPLE
are in such utter darkness,
they will **burn** you

just to see
a **light**.

13

II.   CALL TO ACTION

'[…] there comes a time when one must take a position that is neither safe, nor politic, nor popular, but he must take it because conscience tells him it is right.'

Dr Martin Luther King Jr

WAR ON SILENCE

Always ask yourself: 'What will happen if I say nothing?'

Let our silence grow with noise
as pregnant mothers grow with life.
Let our silence permeate these walls
as sunlight permeates a house.

Let the silence rise from unwatered graves
and craters left by bombs.
Let the silence rise from empty bellies
and surge from broken hearts.

The silence of the hidden and forgotten.
The silence of the battered and tortured.
The silence of the persecuted and imprisoned.
The silence of the hanged and massacred.

Loud as all the sounds can be,
let our silence be loud
so the hungry may eat our words,
and the poor may wear our words.

Loud as all the sounds can be,
let our silence be loud
so we may resurrect the dead
and give voice to the oppressed.

Our silence speaks.

HALF-LIFE

Do not succumb to the half-life,
to the indifference and apathy
of those cool and aloof individuals.
Nothing affects them.
Their lovers desperately cry
out for affection,
but they shrug their shoulders,
for they are always shrugging,
and transcend the messy drama
of the human situation.
Oh, this transcendental invincibility—
        the shit of the bull!
Even Christ chose immanence
so He could feel as the people felt,
suffer as they did.
You must revel in your neuroses,
your sensitivities and sensibilities.
Burn your excitable characters.
Do not extinguish this fire. Stay within.
Taste the immediacy of living.
Be in life with others.
Do not yield to the hypocrisy
the world demands!
Do not succumb to the shadows,
to the half-life, the half-light.
We are not gods.
           Be human.

IF
you wait until you find
something appropriate
to speak up for,
something convenient
that directly concerns you
and attacks your beliefs,

THEN
eventually,
when the day arrives,
you might also find
you have forgotten
how to s p e a k.

—and should I have the right to smile?

Isn't it strange
that in order to be happy
we have to disregard
all the sadness in the world?
That we have to overlook the ballooned
bellies of children, which are dark
and empty inside. That not too far
from our warm homes, the elderly sleep
on cardboard. That there are teenagers
trained to carry heavy rifles,
but their nightmares compel them
to aim the weapon
at themselves.
That there are battered dogs
with skin taut like a drum
and ribs jutting out—their eyes
so beautiful
it makes all the men cry.
Isn't it strange that in order to be happy
we have to unremember
what we already know?
                    And yet,
maybe we aren't meant
to pursue happiness
despite
all the sadness.
                    Maybe,
it's a call for us
to help others instead.

POLISH
the mirror of your heart
until it reflects
every person's light.

SITTING IN THE COURTYARD,
I watch the woman sweeping.
I luxuriate in the sound
of the bristles of her besom
against the ground. She sweeps
in an invisible pattern only she
understands. I study her hands.
They are blackened with chimney dust—
not unlike the soft dust she's now sweeping.
It rises in a cloud above her, which makes me
wonder: *Where does it come from?*
The dust on our overworked hands and travelled
shoes. The dust we inhale and cough
into our handkerchiefs.
The house dust, the road dust, the concrete dust,
and cosmic dust. *Where are they born?*
Perhaps they come from our aged bodies.
We shed our skins like we shed our beauty—
not all at once.
And we walk freely on this blanket of dust
without paying any mind to our ancestors,
though we walk on them! Tread softly,
for you tread on Yeats's wrists and Poe's
elbows. You tread on van Gogh's ears
and Keller's eyes. You breathe
in your grandfather's lover and the little girl
you were when you were four. You smell them
after the first rain in a long dry spell,
or when an old lamp smoulders the bulb quite well.
These all serve as reminders
of our dusty secret:
we are all dust
under
dust under
dust.
     So next time it settles,
                     remember to ask the dust!

I LEFT THE BANK,
for they wouldn't deposit
my cheque of poems.
I went to the store,
but they declined
my currency of words.
I boxed all my stories
and gave them to charity,
yet they refused my gift
and asked me to give blood
instead.
I opened my books
and made them look:
What do you think
I wrote these in?

III.   SONGS OF HOPE

*'You can cut all the flowers but you cannot keep
Spring from coming.'*

Pablo Neruda

COME, FRIENDS.
Come with your grief.
Come with your loss.

Carry all the pieces of your heart
and come sit with us.

Bring your regrets
and your failures.
Bring your betrayals
and your masks.

We welcome you no matter
where you come from
and what you bring.

Come and join us
at the intersection
of acceptance and forgiveness,
where you will find
our house of love.

Bring your empty cups,
and we will have a feast.

BE LIKE THE SUN
that fell in love with the moon
and shared all its light.

Be like the moon
that became a lighthouse
to guide others in the night.

Be like the mountains
that were once hills
wanting to kiss the sky.

Be like the trees
that are firmly grounded
but dream up high.

Be like the waves
that tease and tickle
each other endlessly.

Be like the children
who live and revel
in the present entirely.

Be like the God
that equally loves
everything and everyone.

And be like the love
that brought compassion
when it visited the sun.

LET US GO

Let us go where skins are rainbows,
enriched by every hue.

Where genders are clouds,
weightless and formless through.

Let us go where creeds are stars,
illuminating our view.

Where men and women are one,
and the in-betweens are true.

Let us go where I am free to love,
for I cannot unlove you.

MY WORLD

My world is full of beauty,
but you avert your eyes.

My world is full of light,
but you only worship the dark.

My world is filled with song,
but you exalt silence.

My world is filled with delight,
but you cut throats that ring with laughter.

My world is adorned with exquisite art,
but you smash sculptures,
destroying ancient civilisations.

In my world,
people rejoice with one another
and share each other's burdens,
but you only preach vanity and greed.

What do you know of courage?
What do you know of resilience?

My world is so vast,
it welcomes even you—
for your drop of hatred
will always be absolved
in our ocean of love.

A PART OF US REMAINS

when we leave somewhere.
It is a part we can never reclaim
even if we revisit the place,
for it was never ours to begin with.
There is so little of us
that belongs to ourselves.
This body is the earth's.
This heart is yours,
and hers, and theirs.
The only thing that is our own
is our freedom of will—
the freedom to choose
our perceptions in life.
All else is borrowed.
All else is everyone else's.

CITIES

Lisbon, to me,
is the Lisbon of Pessoa.
Just like London is Woolf's,
or rather, Mrs Dalloway's.
Barcelona is Gaudí's
and Rome is da Vinci's.
You see them in every crevice
and hear their echo
in every cathedral.
I'd like to be the child,
or rather, the mother
of a city.
But I neither have a home
nor a resting place.
My race is humankind.
My religion is kindness.
My work is love,
and, well, my city
is the walls of your heart.

YOU, OVER THERE.

You, who's always looking
over his neighbour's fence.
The beauty of this world is wasted on you.
I say, the beauty of this world
is wasted on you.
You use your eyes to cast disapproving looks.
You use your tongue to degrade and denigrate.
And worst of all, you use your dirty hands
to reach into pockets,
thinking happiness is found
in coins.
But happiness is the bird
that will never fly near you,
because it knows your desire to cage it—
like you do with everything else.
You cage love so two men can't share it.
You cage hope because you can't stand faith.
And you cage God so people think darkness
is all there is.
But the only thing you've successfully caged
is your petty mind.
I need you to know one thing:
There will never be a cage to confine
our light!
We, here, we are free.
        Free to dream.
                Free to love.
                        And free to be
                                who we want to be.

NOTE TO SELF:

even if you spend your life reading the greatest books,
listening to the most divine classical music, & getting
drunk on stunning vistas of mountains & waterfalls, all
of it is meaningless if you aren't sharing it with
someone. everything amounts to that. true, we must
experience some things in solitude in order to grow,
create, destroy, & grow again, but our pleasure & joy
reach a threshold in isolation. it is the worst thing to
become

                                          an island.

one must become the whole world.

TODAY IS A WRITING DAY.
My head is spinning with rapture
as the words rise from my throat.
I am dizzy
from holding the world in my palm.
At dusk, my lantern and I go
in search of cries of the destitute,
the displaced,
and dispossessed.
I lend them my pen
and offer them my heart.

Today is a sacred day.
My skin is anointed with their blood,
and I am ready to battle the darkness.
With hope as my shield
and love as my sword,
I will not return until dawn.
Because no one must be forgotten.
Because victory is possible.
Because anything is possible,
for today is a writing day.

WRITERS AREN'T ALCHEMISTS who transmute the human experience into aurous words. No, writers are glaziers, placing glass onto windows of stories that enable us to see inside. And if they are really good, we can see our own reflections staring back at us.

WHEN I AM GONE,
break the night.
Set my remains on fire
so I can still be your light,
for I am forever indebted to you.
O people of the world,
O love,
          I am eternally yours.

38

## IV.	ECHOES OF HOPE

'Spring has returned.
The Earth is like a child that knows poems.'

Rainer Maria Rilke

I am not separate from you, my neighbour.
If you are my enemy,
then I am my own enemy.
If you are my friend,
then I am my own friend.
Today, I have stripped off my masks
and come to know myself.
I am Christian. I am Jew.
I am Muslim and Hindu.
I am European and African,
Asian and South American.
I am man. I am woman. I am two-spirit.
I am gay. I am asexual. I am straight.
I am abled. I am disabled.
I am all these things because you are,
and you are all these things because we are.
I exist in relation to each of you—
this is what gives my being meaning.
Why must I label myself like a bottle of wine?
When I am the bottle, the wine,
and drunkenness.
Why must I label myself at all?
When I am the flesh, the light, and the shadow.
When I am the voice, the song, and the echo.
Tell me why I must label myself
when I am the lover, the beloved, and love.
I am not separate from you, my neighbour.
And you are not separate from humanity.
We are all mirrors,
reflecting one another
in perpetuity.

ODE TO LIFE

I

This is an ode to life.
The anthem of the world.
For as there are billions of stars
that make up the sky,
so, too, are there billions of humans
that make up the Earth.
Some shine brighter,
but all are made of the same
cosmic dust.
Oh, the joy of being
in life with all these people!

II

I speak of differences
because they exist,
like the different organs
that make up our bodies.
Earth, itself, is one large body.
Listen to how it howls
when a human is in misery.
When one kills another,
Earth feels the pangs in its chest.
When one orgasms,
Earth craves a cigarette.
Look carefully,
these animals are freckles
that make Earth's face lovelier
and more loveable.
These oceans are Earth's limpid eyes.
These trees, its hair.

III

This is an ode to life.
The anthem of the world.
I will no longer speak of differences,
for the similarities are greater.
Look closer. There may be distances
between our limbs,
but there are no spaces
betweenourhearts.
We long to be one.
We long to be in nature
and run wild with its wildlife.
Let us celebrate life and living,
for it is sacrilegious to be ungrateful.
Let us play and be playful,
for it is blasphemous to be serious.
Let us celebrate imperfections
and make existence proud of us,
for tomorrow is death—
and this is an ode to life.
The anthem of the world.

WE DON'T FIND GOD
in temples and cathedrals.
We don't find Her
by standing on a prayer rug
or sitting in a pew.
God appears when we love
—and we feel Her presence
when we help one another.
Because God is not found
in mosques and synagogues.
She resides in our hearts.

LET US GIVE THANKS
for our shadows—
they exist in the first place
because of the presence of light.

CELEBRATION

This is a day of celebration!
Today, we are divorcing the past
and marrying the present.
Dance,
and you will meet God
in every room.
Today, we are divorcing resentment
and marrying forgiveness.
Sing,
and God will greet you
in every tune.
Today, we are divorcing indifference
and marrying love.
Drink, and play that tambourine
against your thigh.
We have so much celebrating to do!

FIND ME HERE,
said love.
I will wait for you
below and above.

I will wait for you
in the dark, in the light.
I will wait for you
in the day, in the night.

I have waited millions of years
and haven't grown weary once.
All of eternity I will wait,
though there's nowhere I haven't been once.

I have been in hearts and groins,
in the whole and the chasm.
I have been in birth and death,
in the cries and the orgasm.

If you close your eyes, I am there
in your nakedness, in your truth.
If you ask for me, I will come
in your age, in your youth.

Because I love you, lover,
and wish to be loved.
Find me here, said love.
I wish to be loved.

NAME	AND	FORM
are	simply	illusions
of		separation.
Love		doesn't
make		us
blind;		rather,
it		erases
the		illusions
so		we
can		see

clearly.

THEY TOOK MY BOOKS
because my message was love.
Then they took my pen
because my words were love.
They took my voice
because my speech was love.
And soon, they'll take me too
so nothing remains.
But they don't know
that when I'm gone,

my love will stay.

Thank you for purchasing *God, Does Humanity Exist?*
Reading is important at every age because it cultivates
the greatest human quality—empathy. However,
we should not have to destroy our environment
in order to create books. By purchasing this book, you
have helped pay for one tree to be planted in Sub-
Saharan Africa, providing families with food, income,
and education, and thereby advocating empowerment
and sustainability.

ACKNOWLEDGMENTS

This book exists because of my father.

A special thank you to my world, my twin sister.

Thank you to my mother and brothers for their continual support.

Thank you to Mehrnoosh Izadi, Daniel Saison, Bahram Zamani, Farshid Kojouri, Sara Javadi, Armen Nazarian, Laura Lentz, Nico J. Genes, Rhea Seren Phillips, Supoorna Kulatunga, Markus Ebrahim, Rana Choudhury, Andrew Terris, James P. Graham, Ayn Gailey, Sara Farish, Zachary J. Moore, Gregg Louis Taylor, and John Goodby.

Thank you to George for being my light and making me feel light.

And last, but certainly not least, a heartfelt thank you to all those who take the time to reach out to me and encourage me with their kinds words. It means so much to me. Thank you.

Kamand Kojouri was born in Tehran, raised in Dubai and Toronto, and resides in Wales. Her first book, *The Eternal Dance: Love Poetry and Prose*, was published in 2018. She currently teaches creative writing seminars as a doctoral candidate at Swansea University.

Printed in Great Britain
by Amazon

36482842R00038